A Nation Divided by Racism

A Nation Divided by Racism

Patrick Baker

J. Kenkade
PUBLISHING®

Little Rock, Arkansas

J. Kenkade Publishing
6104 Forbing Rd
Little Rock, AR 72209
www.jkenkadepublishing.com
Facebook.com/jkenkadepublishing
J. Kenkade Publishing is a registered trademark.

Printed in the United States of America
ISBN 978-1-944486-54-9

Acknowledgements

First, I would like to thank the Lord God, almighty Creator of Heaven and Earth, who has inspired me to write this book. I thank Him for the encouragement to write this book even when I know that it will change some people who read it, and it will make some people hate more. I know that all things are in your hands and even when it doesn't seem like it.

I acknowledge both of my parents, Linda and Jerry Baker Jr., for being the parents that God has given me, and for raising me the best they could and instilling in me the values of life at an early age and steering me in the direction of Christ.

I thank you, Lord, for the inspiration to be outspoken when I am provoked to be silent. Your grace has brought humanity a long way from where we first started as a nation and for that we give your name all the praise and glory!

-Amen

Land of the Free

◆ ◆ ◆

This nation was built on the sweat, tears, and blood of African Americans for so many years. America was not always the land of the free; freedom has always come with a high ransom in the form of beatings or even death. Imagine being held like property, only able to go and come at the direction of your property owner, and worked to death for pennies only to make another person rich. We, as a diverse nation of people (and, further, as a whole as a human race), are so divided because we don't want to accept the differences in people.

We don't want to accept anything that we don't understand because what we don't understand challenges us.

As people, we are so misguided because of the colors of our skin. We live in a nation of laws that are being overlooked every day depending on the color of one's skin. America should be a beacon of light shining to the rest of the world, but that light is being snuffed and smothered out because of racism and hatred. Some people are so set in their ways that they would rather die and go to Hell than live and be unified.

This is not the land of the free, no matter how much I love this great nation and the recourse God gave us when he sent his son Jesus Christ to die for our sins. Only through the knowledge of Christ do we truly become free even in the middle of a hostile nation ("If the Son therefore shall make you free, ye shall be free indeed," John 8:36).

In order to fix a problem, you have to start with the root of the problem or the reason for the problem. We're not living by America's creed: "I pledge allegiance to the flag of the United States of America, and to the Republic for which it stands, one nation under God, indivisible with liberty and justice for all."

No matter how we look at it, justice comes in the form of color and liberation only comes after death. Everything that is done today is just modified, from newer prisons to more policing in black neighborhoods, to open-and-carry. All of these are tactics for justification. Most black people work nine-to-five jobs, and the first thing is taking taxes, from Medicare to social security, to state taxes, but minimum wage is only $7.25 an hour. So, in that way, we are being held as property in poverty. This government will not raise minimum wage but will raise food and gas prices.

We are living in a country where it is normal to be harassed by the police just because you are viewed differently for having a different skin color.

We are seen as inferior because of being stigmatized from the gruesome past of our ancestors. The prison systems today are built for the black man. They put more police patrolling our neighborhoods because we as a people lack the understanding to know a setup. We don't understand how to become unified as a race that keeps the black man suppressed by the system. ("[There is] one Lord, one faith, one baptism, One God and Father of all, who is above all, and through all, and in you all," Ephesians 4:5-6).

Even today, we live in a world where if we don't share the same point of view, whether it be personal or political, we are sent hate messages, such as dolls with strings around their necks or burning crosses placed in our yards. It is because the stem of racism, even the core root or seed, is hatred. Racism simply stems from a depth of hatred.

Unless we allow Christ in our hearts to fix us as individual people, we will not be fixed as a nation.

However, so often, as black people, we ourselves are being engulfed by this glamorous material lifestyle that has imprisoned our thinking, and we're almost willing to do anything to obtain it, from stealing to robbery to assault and domestic violence, and even to murder. We have to start by trying to become better individuals before we can become a united race. We are continually trying to take shortcuts in life, trying to obtain worldly wealth in ways that are hurting us as a race, from selling drugs to robbery, and so on. No race will respect us until we respect ourselves, until we as a race can pull up our pants, walk in the self-respect and dignity of our ancestors, who paid the ultimate price for us so that we might have what they believed was justice for us as people– being equal to our Caucasian brothers and sisters. However, we will always be viewed as inferior because respect is earned, not given. They tell us black Americans the reason that there are more police patrolling our neighborhoods is because there is more crime.

That is a setup.

If the government can control other neighborhoods without excessive policing, then why can't they make our neighborhoods like theirs? Why is there so much less gentrification in black neighborhoods? They build these low-income houses in projects and ghettos where tenants still have to pay equal or higher rent with no modifications, and the qualifications for this type of housing are based upon low-income status. We are forced to live in low-class income housing like we are on some modern-day plantation, with "one way in and one way out" driveways, which makes us as black people feel as though we are being trapped in cages, so were mostly compelled to become what we see in projects and ghettos.

You rarely see these people going to work for companies in suits and ties.

So often they are in white tees and Dickies, working the corner, and the reason for this is because you understand what survival is when you see your parents struggling to support their family in low-income jobs because of lack of education from working in cotton fields and not being able to go to school.

We are also governed by this new law of open-and-carry. This law is only for white Americans to politicize their second amendment constitutional right, just another scheme to say the black man is resisting or had a weapon, and the white man feared for his life. So many people have been beaten to death or shot without a weapon. Why wouldn't you think this law would make it worse? We live in a world where we play chess, not checkers. Every law that is passed is just another way to remove a pawn from the board because we live in a world today where if we are even able to get a higher education by going to college as a minority, then most of us have to get grants and student loans just to graduate, and then may not even find a job in our fields of study, but we are still left paying back grants or loans with interest for half of our lives. That means it costs more to go to school in the long run. We as black people need to realize that the constitution was not made for black people. Then we realize that we live in a divided nation. The only law that has ever been passed for black people was the Emancipation Proclamation, which allowed for us to actually start being seen as people and not as property.

We've always used what we had to make the best life for our families.

If we were fast, we ran track. If we could jump, shoot, or dribble, we played basketball. If we were strong, we played football. If we could harmonize, we made music.

All of these avenues are mostly dominated by African Americans, and that shows us that when you use the gift that God has given, it always opens the door for provision. We have come so far as a race, but we still have a way to go to be united as a nation. We are the light of the world. We are God's people. Just as well as you can hate, you can love. It's a choice. The constant fear our fellow Americans have about us as black Americans is that if we have too many resources, we would somehow try to do them the way they did us, but all we want is to be treated like people and not be killed just for being black.

There are many after-school programs for white kids like YMCA, Girl Scouts, and Boy Scouts, but in the black communities, there are no after-school activities– no Boys and Girls Clubs where you train kids early to tap into their gifts and teach them how to become young men and women, children of character and morals. We are coming up as African American kids being raised by single parents because so many men are falling into the hands of the system, which deprives their sons of becoming men who take accountability and responsibility.

When you make a kid, you don't leave it for the world to raise.

You instill the possibility of greatness into them so that they can withstand the tactics of the adversary, which is Satan ("Be sober, be vigilant; because your adversary the devil, as a roaring lion, walketh about, seeking whom he may devour:" 1 Peter 5:8).

We need to understand that as a whole we're either going to be vessels for Christ or Satan, good or evil, because if we won't come together ourselves, we've seen in the past that catastrophic events will be what unite us as a people. Our nation has endured so much to try to go back to where we started. When we stop viewing people who don't look like us as a threat, then we will be able to live united as people.

Not every Mexican is a drug dealer or a rapist. Not every Muslim is a terrorist. Not every black man is a gang-banger.

While grace has been given to humanity as a whole, justice is selective. We are mostly misguided in thinking that these laws that are being passed and those that have been passed are for African Americans. Although we live in the same country, we have two different life experiences, depending on the colors of our skin. My version of this great country that my people have gone into war to fight for is hot sweating in cotton fields, segregated schools and restaurants, and being treated like animals, while lighter-skinned Americans are given the first of everything, the best of everything, the most of everything.

The political diplomats who are supposed to be the voice of the people are using politics for monetary gain, which only benefits lawmakers because– let's be honest– there isn't anyone who has never broken the law, but not everyone who has broken the law has been punished.

As people, instead of dealing with a problem, we would rather look past it and act as if there is no problem, and, as a nation, that's how we look at racism. Instead of America sitting down and having a serious dialogue about racism, we would rather act as though it doesn't exist because we don't want to ruffle anyone's feathers.

We can never make America great again because America was never great.

The slogan "Make America Great Again" is just a silent statement to racist, white Americans that the aim for this country is to put African Americans back in their place. So many times, we hear vague statements like that that might not have gotten as much publicity but have the same meaning because making America "great again" for African Americans would be going back to the back of the bus, drinking at broken water fountains, going back into the cotton fields, and being demoralized as human beings. So that statement couldn't have been for any African American.

Until we have someone in office who can unify us as people, we will never be unified as a nation.

The fact is that, as Americans, we're all supposed to have every equality as human beings, but the truth of the matter is that often times we're not even seen as human beings. So often, we are still being looked at as property, only now it's by managers, COOs, and CEOs letting us know that even though they've given us a little headway, we should still stay in our "place", meaning if you speak out for morality using your platform, then you are not being patriotic to the country or you're disrespecting the flag.

When someone, as a fellow American, can turn and look away from hatred, racism, and bigotry without exposing them, their America is not my America.

When we are allowed to be divided as people, we allow room for hatred to arise. Hatred is the head of violence, and, as you know, behind violence is death. Until we can put our personal differences aside, let our past become our lesson, and become unified, we will not be great as a nation or as people.

The time will come where we will be tested, and how we treat people is what makes this great country stand out from other countries. When we make the decision to stand up for what is right and stop looking over wrong, we will make a start to becoming unified ("…Every kingdom divided against itself is brought to desolation; and every city or house divided against itself shall not stand: And if Satan cast out Satan, he is divided against himself; how shall then his kingdom stand?" Matthew 12:25-26).

As long as there are humans, there will be a spirit of division among us.

As human beings, the reason that so much hatred is among us is because we failed to retain Jesus Christ as a part of our everyday journey. This war that we are fighting is not physical but rather spiritual. Until we realize what weapon to use and when to use it, we will constantly be destroyed by the adversary ("For we wrestle not against flesh and blood, but against principalities, against powers, against the rulers of the darkness of this world, against spiritual wickedness in high places," Ephesians 6:12).

Instead of putting guns in teachers' hands, put the Bible back in the classrooms and have prayer before classes like the days before when you never heard of a school shooting. We are being so engulfed and distracted by political war from different political points of views that we are forgetting the reason they exist. It is not for one's own personal agenda that he or she has been elected into office, but rather to govern his or her state, and, as the president, to govern the country, so his or her focus should be on what is best for the people. We are seeing so much division among the American people because there are no real examples to show the world true unification. Until we can look past our personal differences and come together as people, this country is slowly slipping into the past perception of people, which is deadly ("Neither do people pour new wine into old wineskins. If they do, the skins will burst; the wine will run out and the wineskins will be ruined. No, they pour new wine into new wineskins, and both are preserved," Matthew 9:17, NIV). This means you cannot do to this generation what was once done to our ancestors because their train of thought was very different. It is only when the passion for love and righteousness is deeper than the hatred that so boldly embodies us that we will see progress.

Just because my skin color is different does not mean that my personal morals are any lower.

We have kids, too, and we just want the lives for our children that we never had. We are being shot down in the streets by police, the ones who are supposed to be protecting and serving our community, after being targeted as bad people for not having the same chances as our fellow Americans. We are being discriminated against daily, even losing our jobs, because they feel that we are at the bottom of the totem pole. Being less fortunate doesn't matter to them. We are being led astray, whether willingly or begrudgingly giving in to the hatred that is woven so deeply within every strand of our DNA that makes us hate our fellow Americans.

Whatever the reason, we have to become better people and then better Americans.

Life is a gift that should be cherished and enjoyed with love, laughter, peace, and joy, not with hatred, racism, bigotry, and self-destruction. It is easy to hate, kill, and be destructive, but it takes work to love because true love acknowledges a power that's higher than self. Our differences are what separate us as individuals, but our love is what brings us together as a nation.

This nation should be identified by the love that we share. Instead, we are being guided by fear and driven by hatred.

We are afraid of the darkness within ourselves (There is no fear in love; but perfect love casteth out fear: because fear hath torment. He that feareth is not made perfect in love," 1 John 4:18). This nation is driven by greed, power, and wealth, which are the core values of any nation, but we show our true character when we do what is right by all people. Why would we have the power to subdue our adversaries if we can't walk the streets safely in this country or drive without the fear of being killed at the hands of a police officer or a rebel flying down the street with his shotgun and a confederate flag, screaming "White America!"?

If this continues, we will never be great.

We will be the same divided America that we've always been. Not only for America, but for the world, biblical prophecy is being fulfilled. The hour for such things to take place is happening; this is the appointed hour for them. As people, it is easy to sit back, lay blame, and point fingers, but when do we as human beings start becoming self-aware and conscious of our own faults and mistakes? When we do that, we will start to preserve the life of mankind. When we accept the responsibility of our wrongs and mistakes, then and only then will we be able to start to work on ourselves. Freedom is for everyone, and justice for all. There is no more room for us as people who know right from wrong, who swear men and women into office by the Holy Bible to uphold what is right and renounce what is wrong, to think that they will not go unpunished because of their position ("Understand, ye brutish among the people:

and ye fools, when will you be wise? He that planted the ear, shall he not hear? He that formed the eye, shall he not see? He that chastiseth the heathen, shall not he correct? He that teacheth man knowledge, shall not he know? The Lord knoweth the thoughts of man, that they are vanity," Psalms 94:8-11).

There will come a time when the people who are able to enact justice and righteousness but don't because of hatred or monetary gain will be judged rightfully.

In America, we act as though we lack the understanding of unity. We are not really comfortable unless we are in our own little groups because socializing with people outside of our own ethnicity groups makes us have to survey ourselves. This nation is only considered great depending upon the values it upholds. How is it that we can use the Holy Bible to swear people into office, which shows that America believes in a higher power, as well as acknowledge that Jesus Christ is the son of God and we believe that God is the Supreme Being, but we cannot retain God in everything that we do in America? ("Therefore, anyone who swears by the altar swears by it and everything on it. And anyone who swears by the temple swears by it and by the one who dwells in it. And anyone who swears by heaven swears by God's throne and by the one who sits on it," Matthew 23:20-21, NIV).

Life as an American can be so difficult, depending on the color of your skin. Some of us didn't get good starts in life, which makes it even more difficult to survive and support our families because we struggle to do what should be so natural as humans, and that is to love each other. America is in so much political uproar, and there is so much division within the legislative branch of the government, that we as Americans can't even come together to make laws that benefit all Americans.

We are lost as a nation, and the only way we will be restored as a nation is to allow the love of Christ in our hearts.

We are living in a world where we look over wrong-doing depending on who the person is and give praise to everyone except who we really should be praising ("Render therefore to all their dues: tribute to whom tribute is due; custom to whom custom; fear to whom fear; honour to whom honour," Romans 13:7).

So why we are trying to make America great again when it never was great? We should be trying to make the world great again by doing right by all nations and all people, regardless of race, religion, or political affiliation. A widely held view by our past leaders and social activists is that you cannot fight hate with hate ("Anyone who claims to be in the light but hates a brother or sister is still in the darkness," 1 John 2:9, NIV). My personal family members went to wars and fought for my freedom, as well as the freedom of my fellow Americans, which gives me the freedom and the right to address certain unethical, immoral, blatant hypocrisy of some Americans. This kind of hypocrisy causes more division than unification, and some of the rights I possess because of this are freedom of speech and freedom of the press.

That's why I'm writing this book and addressing these matters – I will not sit back and watch this nation treat people with certain skin colors or religious backgrounds like they are not human beings. All of this has been foretold long before these things started happening, beginning in the book of Matthew ("And ye shall hear of wars and rumours of wars: see that ye be not troubled: for all these things must come to pass, but the end is not yet. For nation shall rise against nation, and kingdom against kingdom: and there shall be famines, and pestilences, and earthquakes, in divers places. All these things are the beginning of sorrows," Matthew 24:6-8). We are seeing disasters in every part of the world, from Hurricanes Harvey, Michael, and Florence, to the Middle Eastern Wars in Aleppo, to terrorist attacks in Paris, to severe earthquakes in Iran, Iraq, Nepal, Papua New Guinea, and Indonesia, erupting volcanoes in Hawaii, as well as tension between North Korea and the U.S., tension between Japan and the U.S., and controversial relations between Russia and the United States.

These things are happening to this day. Terror has no color, and hatred is a quickly spreading virus. Famine is so severe in some countries in the world. Racism is a demonic spirit that takes hold of any individual who will allow themselves to become a vessel.

This nation is in such turmoil because we as people cannot have a difference of opinion as adults (When I was a child, I spake as a child, I understood as a child, I thought as a child: but when I became a man, I put away childish things," 1 Corinthians 13:11). See, there are too many adults in serious positions who are still speaking and understanding as children, and it is perpetuating chaos among the American people. It is a tactic by the adversary so that he can pick off the weak because there is strength in numbers. It hurts me personally to see everything around me evolve in this way, to look at the human race and see how we would rather stay the same and return to our wicked ways like a dog returning to its vomit.

This nation is decomposing every day like a dead body because of the lack of preservation for humanity. We as people don't have the answers to why we are so divided and why we're only able to reason with our own race because we look for empathy and sympathy, and we know that we are able to get it from the people who look like us. But when we see the plight of others, we see that perhaps things are not as bad as they seem. When people are being slaughtered because of the color of their skin or their personal spiritual belief, you know something more powerful is at work within. This is inhuman, as well as unnatural.

It seems that the more we know what is unnatural or not right, the more we seem to indulge in it, like same-sex marriages, bisexuality, and lesbianism. We know inside out that these are not right and unnatural, but we still try to override the word of God ("For this cause God gave them up unto vile affections: for even their women did change the natural use into that which is against nature: And likewise also the men, leaving the natural use of the woman, burned in their lust one toward another; men with men working that which is unseemly, in receiving in themselves that recompence of their error which was meet. And even as they did not like to retain God in their knowledge, God gave them over to a reprobate mind, to do those things which are not convenient; Being filled with all unrighteousness, fornication, wickedness, covetousness, maliciousness; full of envy, murder, debate, deceit, malignity; whisperers, Backbiters, haters of God, despiteful, proud, boasters, inventors of evil things, disobedient to parents, Without understanding, covenant breakers, without natural affection, implacable, unmerciful: Who knowing the judgment of God, that they which commit such things are worthy of death, not only do the same, but have pleasure in them that do them," Romans 1:26 -32).

This is not new information; it's just overlooked because we'd rather do what feels good rather than do what is right.

For a lot of the division that we deal with today, every ethnicity group plays a part because of hatred. We cannot change the past; we can only learn from it. So when you decide to be ignorant about the history of America, you are making a decision to repeat history, which is dangerous as a society because certain Americans will do anything to keep from going back to where they came from.

Everybody's scars have a story behind them, whether they are physical, emotional, mental, or spiritual scars.

Every scar that we bear is a reflection of some part of our past or present state of being. How we regard our scars is how we mold our future ("If my people, which are called by my name, shall humble themselves, and pray, and seek my face, and turn from their wicked ways; then will I hear from heaven, and will forgive their sin, and will heal their land," 2 Chronicles 7:14). We have to start with a different outlook for humanity. We have to start by being more conscious of how we treat people as individuals. God has bestowed the gift of life to everything that is living, and if we love life, why do we try to play God by telling certain people what they can do, how they can do it, and when? Why do we treat life like a curse if it's a gift? We have so much hatred in this country that is unreal, and it's not mainly Middle Easterners or people from all these other countries who have been said to be terroristic. In fact, it is often angry, hateful white Americans who feel like their country is somehow being taken from them.

So, instead of them looking at all people as people who are striving for the same causes, freedom and the American dream, which is to support themselves and their families without being harmed in the process, they would rather stay hateful in their own white supremacist groups and spread divisiveness throughout the country.

So, the question now is where do we go from here as a country? Which direction are we really moving in as a nation?

These are personal questions that we should be asking ourselves and answering sincerely. The answers would tell you what part of the country you should be on because obviously we are a divided nation.

With life comes opposition. With understanding comes growth. With growth comes knowledge. With knowledge comes wisdom ("If any of you lack wisdom, let him ask of God, that giveth to all men liberally, and upbraideth not; and it will be given him," James 1:5).

America has shed so much innocent blood silently, which will inevitably cause a ripple effect throughout generations to come. That is why we are witnesses of so much terror, such as the murders in Nevada, Florida, and California, two of which were school shootings involving kids. This is the ripple effect of wrongdoing in this country. We want to point fingers and blame instead of looking for positive solutions. We want to pretend that these things did not happen. However, the families of all the victims, everyone who has lost a loved one, and every one of these cities knows how real this is because they feel the pain from it every day. They wake up in the morning and lay down at night and don't see the ones that they love because of an emotional trigger that was set off within every one of these shooters because of the hate within them for other mankind. We look for reasons to dislike or even hate people because they are different, and we laugh and make fun of other students because their parents can't afford things that other parents are able to afford for their kids. It starts at an early age for kids to build up hatred towards people. We have to become better stewards over what God has put in our possession because God can easily take back what He has put us in charge of.

Humans have become so arrogant because we act as if we have the right to make others answer to us, who are also mere humans.

We cannot treat people as though any race or any individual owns anything ("The earth is the Lord's, and the fulness thereof; the world, and they that dwell therein," Psalm 24). We will not take anything from this world with us when we leave it. We didn't bring anything with us when we came into it, and that's how we will depart it. God put enough resources on Earth for humanity before He created man, so why is it that there's so much hatred in the hearts of certain people when they see people of other ethnicities prosper?

When you possess resources such as currency or capital, those should be considered resources you can use to make an impact.

You can change things.

That's why these politicians don't want NFL players saying anything because they know that people will listen, so they threaten them by trying to put in place certain laws that prevent them from speaking out. The most important tool God gave humanity is a voice, so you can either create darkness or condemn darkness and bring light to dark places, depending on what comes out of your mouth ("Let no corrupt communication proceed out of your mouth, but that which is good to the use of edifying, that it may minister grace unto the hearers," Ephesians 4:29). America is being governed by systemic racism and quiet oppression, and this is just where we are as a country. As bad as it sounds, this is American society, but no one wants to admit it because admitting it means we would have to deal with the problem, so we would rather be quiet and continue living in darkness. We are destined to answer for the decision that this country has made against God's people just because of racial differences. We will all have to answer to God as individuals ("For we must all appear before the judgment seat of Christ; that every one may receive the things done in his body, according to that he hath done, whether it be good or bad," 2 Corinthians 5:10). Everyone has to answer for the life they have lived.

We as humans are ignorant to life, living in the world's dark abyss of worldly gain and what we call the pursuit of happiness, only to realize when we achieve it that it's not things or money that truly make us happy.

True happiness come from within, so when we start being able to look at one another as God sees us, which is all as human beings, then we will start to understand how to truly love and treat one another.

Life was given by God to be enjoyed, full of love, innocence, and worship, in communion with the creator. But we have perverted it with disobedience, anger, discord, and, most of all, hatred. We have all been given another chance by the grace of God through the bloodshed of his son, my Lord and Savior Jesus Christ. How severe a blow do you think it is to God when we reject such grace? ("How much more severely do you think someone deserves to be punished who has trampled the Son of God underfoot, who has treated as an unholy thing the blood of the covenant that sanctified them, and who has insulted the Spirit of grace?" Hebrews 10:29). Jesus Christ has given us one single command in the New Testament – "A new commandment I give unto you, That ye love one another; as I have loved you, that ye also love one another," John 13:34).

While we don't have to share the same opinions or points of view, we do have to share the love of God with everyone.

Anything other than that is sin, so we have to be mindful of how we treat people, as well as how we talk to people, to keep from falling into the snare that the adversary tries to use to manipulate us. So many of us have taken the bait, from accepting bribes, to carrying out extortion or blackmail, and even to committing murder. We live in a world where one is judged according to their financial status or earthly possessions rather than their character on morality as a person. We do not uphold the true value of humans because we are blinded by worldly possessions; that's why we as humans have no respect for each other as people, and the only way that we can see this is to get closer to the One who created us all.

We did not create ourselves.

We bear the master seal.

There is no division in the trinity of God, and we have similitude with our Creator. We know God did not create us to punish us or divide us, but to have communion with His creation.

This nation opposes every proclamation from the Creator of how we were created and what we were created for. No one person wants to eat or wear the same thing every day. We love having a variety to choose from, so why don't we look at it from a godly point of view?

Why don't we see that our Creator is the author of variety? He creates what pleases Him, like the trees, grass, animals, fruits, vegetables, and humans. When God created Caucasians, Africans, Mexicans, Middle Easterners, and all the rest, he created us differently because he loves variety.

He did not create us for division.

Just because you have a different shade of skin, it does not mean I should look at you as any less of a person because the One who created me created you as well. Our words stir up strife and hatred. What we say to each other divides us from each other ("Death and life are in the power of the tongue: and they that love it shall eat the fruit thereof," Proverbs 18:21).

So why we are going from race to race, spreading toxicity by speaking badly about different ethnicities? We as individuals are spreading this, as well. It's not only by people with platforms, even though they are the most influential. We have to have the audacity to make a stand, look hatred in the eye, and disallow it to continue going from generation to generation and race to race, setting the course of life on fire. We are decimating our children's futures with our current actions. Why do we subscribe to quotes like "Only the strong survive"? We rarely hold on to quotes like "One nation under God, with liberty and justice for all" because those quotes bring unity. Why do we allow quotes like "Only the strong survive" to separate us by race?

Most of the time, how we are treated is mainly determined by our strengths or accomplishments rather than being looked at equally, even though we bear our failures and faults and just want to legitimately be looked at as individual human beings.

Life is irreplaceable, and you only get one chance to get it right.

The way we think has serious repercussions on our lives because change doesn't come until we change the way we think. We can say what we are going to do, we can make New Years' resolutions about how we're going to change certain things, but until one can retrain the way he or she thinks, a situation will never change. That's exactly how it is with America. We won't change, but we want to continually do what America has always done. We're this spectacular country, but we want to keep quiet oppression, systematic suppression, racial injustice, and bigotry, and all this does is take this country back to its flaws, which involved segregation.

Let's be clear and honest – we all know that we've always had a divided nation, and if some Americans could have it their way, we would still be living in the same era.

We are either Americans being pushed to become a better nation or being forced to be the nation that we have always been.

Either way, there is a choice to be made, and what we decide as a nation will determine which direction we are headed. Either way, evolution will make us choose because nothing in this world stays the same– nothing but God ("For I am the Lord, I change not," Malachi 3:6). We often keep the pain of being different bottled up inside of us because of how we were trained to behave, but pain is a natural, physical, and emotional reaction to being hurt. So, if my being different causes you to treat me in a hateful and hostile way, then my natural, psychological reaction is to feel inner pain. No one wants to be mistreated or hurt, no matter the color of their skin. We all just want to be treated as human beings. When we marginalize people, no matter what their religious beliefs, ethnicity, or personal sexual agenda they have, we are using divisive tactics.

I am compelled to speak out about the racial divisiveness of this country because it personally affects me, but I am not the only individual or race representative feeling the effects of this divided country. My darker and lighter shaded Americans are ridiculed and oppressed daily because of where they are from, as well as the shades of their skin. We're not welcoming any other race or ethnicity into this country unless they are of Caucasian descent. When we frown upon any other ethnicity, we are misguided and predatorial. It is so difficult for certain ethnicities to become citizens of this country, a country that was forcefully taken from the Indians, so let's be honest – the only group of people that was here and did not have to travel to get here was the Indians. We all are foreigners in this country.

We all live in our own groups in the world instead of living like one body of people.

We have Caucasians, Chinese, Africans, Mexicans, African Americans, and so on. We have all these different ethnicities that are so diverse. We would all be able to get along with different people if we were able to understand different people, but this country's government only teaches people what it wants them to know. They only want people to learn American history instead of teaching all history. In the 1800s, native war leader "Crazy Horse" came to view Caucasians as terrorists when General Custer led the Seventh Cavalry to kill his community and family and take their land, which is now known as the United States. It's sad to discover all of the misconceptions about America's founders' actions.

Humanity has diverted from its original intent.

America only constitutes laws according to the color of one's skin or nature of ethnic background. It's sad to say that the country my people have fought for so diligently is not the land of the free but still the home of the brave. The senseless reticule that my people have had to endure is from the same people that they went and fought for ("Greater love hath no man than this, that a man lay down his life for his friends," John: 15:13). The division in this country is so prevalent at this very moment that you can feel its existence in the atmosphere. Most immigrants, as well as Americans, seem to be pessimistic about the future of this country because of the indecency and dysfunctional moral compass that this country is guided by ("Behold also the ships, which though they be so great, and are driven of fierce winds, yet are they turned about with a very small helm, whithersoever the governor listeth. Even so the tongue is a little member, and boasteth great things. Behold, how great a matter a little fire kindleth! And the tongue is a fire, a world of iniquity; so is the tongue among our members, that it defileth the whole body, and setteth on fire the course of nature; and it is set on fire of hell," James 3:4-6).

These are not selective accusations but rather live scenarios. This country's treatment of history is to publicize racially motivated monumental statues so that certain Americans can constantly see the injustices as well as feel the horrific disgracefulness and brute hatefulness of where we have been. Sadly, most parts of this country still operate in some of its former ways. The numbers of ethnicities are disproportionate to what this great country is supposed to represent, which is a great, culturally diverse body of people. Moreover, America is supposed to be the pillar of all nations, but when we as a whole are not leading by example, then we are partially to blame for the humanity crisis that is spiraling out of control When do we as a country set aside the divisive attributes that we personally possess and be the leaders we were designed to become? We are preserved for judgment from the creator of all things because of the discord, disobedience, and deceit ("The heart is deceitful above all things, and desperately wicked: who can know it? I the Lord search the heart, I try the reins, even to give every man according to his ways, and according to the fruit of his doings," Jeremiah 17:9-10). Intrinsically, it is only natural for us to question the systematic oppression that is imposed on certain ethnicities.

We are not some scientific experiment that randomly came from the "big bang theory". No, we are a part of God's strategic plan for His purpose. Until we look in the heart of every person, individually seeking his or her good, the light of this country will become dimmer and dimmer until the spirit of darkness takes over. More often than not, the hurt from our past experiences has closed the minds of some Americans because we feel as though we live in a country where our thoughts and feelings are disregarded.

Because of our ethnicities and skin colors, we have been ostracized, brutalized, and humiliated, which has demoralized us as a race to the point that we have lost faith in God.

We feel that somehow He is to blame for the hateful, disgusting, heinous acts that have been done to certain ethnicities, some worse than others. When we take the time to realize what the next group of individuals had to endure just for being who they were, compassion can be doled out by those with understanding because they at some point have been through some of the same tribulations as that group.

No race has had it as bad as Jews or African Americans, who had millions of their races decimated because of hatred. People whose ancestors have gone through widespread trauma can realize the depth of hatred the Holocaust came from – the systematic, bureaucratic, state-sponsored persecution and murder of six million Jews by the Nazi regime and its collaborators.

When the Nazis came into power in Germany in January 1933, they believed that Germans were "racially superior". They claimed that Jews were "inferior" and a threat to the so-called German racial community. By 1945, the Germans and their collaborators killed two out of every three Jews as a part of the "final solution". The "final solution" was the Nazi plan of action to murder the Jews.

During the era of the Holocaust, German authorities also targeted other groups because of their perceived racial and biological inferiority. These included Romani (gypsies), people with disabilities, and others, such as poles, soviet civilians, and blacks. German authorities persecuted other groups on political, ideological, and behavioral grounds. Among them were communist, socialist, Jehovah's Witness, and homosexuals, so instead of identifying one another by our individual ethnicity groups, we as a nation have to understand what we have endured and do what it takes to become a better country when we are challenged by different dialects of different ethnicities.

The cultural foundations of traditional America are being shaken to their core because it is hard for a country that has everything to understand people who come from poverty-stricken countries that are good, decent human beings who just want a better life for their families. We have a deep, widespread humanity crisis, and the reason for that is because we have failed to realize the need to look at people as fellow humans. We fail to see the bigger picture, meaning that until we stop looking at everyone who is not from this country as a threat, we will not solve the ongoing problems.

There should not be one hungry or homeless person in the United States. If we can't take care of our own home, how are we as a country supposed to lead by example? America is supposed to be the heart of diversity and the land of the free. We are crippling our society, as well as our economy, because we are afraid of diversified growth. First, we crippled our society when we denied immigrants because it disallows us to understand different cultural point of views. Secondly, there is a labor market impact. More immigrants mean more hours worked in the economy. Immigration also often boosts labor supply by increasing female labor-force participation via the substantially reduced cost and care services. Thirdly, an increase in skilled migration can directly increase the aggregate level of human capital while low-skilled migration can indirectly boost the supply of labor-force participation of skilled women. Next is the innovation impact.

For the record, knowledge, entrepreneurship, and technology are the driving forces of a dynamic economy. Two reliable ways to generate ideas and innovation in an economy are to increase the number of highly educated workers and introduce diversity into the workplace. Immigrants account for nearly half of the U.S. workforce, with science or engineering doctorates, including 60% of workers in computers and mathematical science.

In Silicon Valley, 64% of engineers are foreign -born, and more than half of us startup "unicorns" have at least one immigrant co-founder. The diversity immigrants bring is also pro-innovation: migrants contribute different points of view than the native population, allowing them to challenge pre-existing business practices, further driving productivity benefits. Immigrants have helped to globally connect capital, talent, and ideas because they bring international connections and are more willing to explore globally, spotting new opportunities and potential innovations. You can also find immigrants in the innovation engines that are our cities: within states, these migrants are also very heavily concentrated often in the most dynamic, urban centers. It is no wonder, then, that a mounting body of evidence points to a negative impact of economic dynamism with lower migrant involvement.

When we deny immigrants entry into this country, we are stunting the growth of our economy, as well as hindering innovative ideas from all around the globe. America deals with the ongoing political backlash from different countries because of trade tariffs, as well as a variety of sanctions that are sometimes good for the country and sometimes less than ideal. This is just some of the political opposition we face as a country. This is just a demonstration of the opposition, which makes it even more difficult to govern and be united as a country because everything that has been done has a major impact on everyday American citizens, from the imports and exports of goods to political shutdowns of the government that have caused so many working government officials not to be able to collect a check. America is so distorted and perilous at this very moment because of emotional politics. The division that America deals with today is terrifying, but we should not despair ("Do not be afraid of those who kill the body but cannot kill the soul. Rather, be afraid of the One Him who can destroy both soul and body in hell," Matthew 10:28). We cannot be divided on every decision we make as a nation, just like we cannot be divided as a nation because of ethnicity, skin tone, or religious beliefs.

We have to understand that we need to love people, treat each other like humans, and get along with each other, even if we disagree on political points of view, or the difference of our ethnic backgrounds, as well as our religious ideologies because that's what brings us together as humans. When we do that, perhaps we will be able to deal with a lot of these ongoing worldwide humanity crises.

This nation is spiraling out of control because of the ones who are creating laws that American citizens are supposed to be governed by but are being broken every day by the ones on Capitol Hill who pass these laws. When you are any other ethnicity than white in a major political position in America, you are held to a higher standard of accountability, not so much because of the position but rather because of who is in the position.

When the leader of the free world can call black male athletes "sons of bitches" because they use formal tactics to speak out about injustices in their communities, there is a widespread problem. When several white celebrities have been accused of some of the same misbehavior as black celebrities like Bill Cosby, such as Bill O'Reilly, Harvey Weinstein, and Kevin Spacey, but the black man is who gets charged in these crimes, there is a widespread problem.

However, no one wants to admit it or talk about it. Cosby's so-called victimizing started around 1965 and continued until 2008. We are being made to believe that when racism was still prevalent and ongoing around that era, women (allegedly white women) were afraid to go to the police and report that they had been assaulted by a black man. That is hard to believe. These are just demonstrations of how divided this country is, and no one really cares about justice as much as they would rather set a precedent. Harsher punishment is given to brown-skinned and darker-skinned people than those who are a lighter shade. African Americans are incarcerated at more than five times the rate of white Americans according to the NAACP criminal justice record. Even though this is statistically factual, most of America would rather facts be disregarded.

We should not give publicity to the names of people who incite racial destruction because it only enables them to become more divisive and destructive.

We as a nation should call it what it is and condemn it because everyone who has eyes, ears, or understanding knows when racism appears. Only the people who condone this behavior ever seem to acknowledge these reprehensible, unpatriotic distractions that are imposed on the American people. This is because if they can distract people from what's really going on, then it's easier to push whatever agenda through that they are trying to get through.

The greatest trick that the devil ever pulled was to make people think that he didn't exist.

There's a difference between illusion and the truth. The danger is in making illusion the truth, meaning if I can get you to believe unsupported, superficial stigma and distort the truth by making you believe illusions of the truth with lies, then I have clearly passed my agenda or imposed my thoughts and beliefs upon you.

We are living in the twenty-first century in a country that's trying so hard to relive history through racism, and, sadly, some people wear racism on their sleeves as a badge of honor because of the immorality and indecency of certain people who feel diversity is disastrous for our nation ("I appeal to you, brothers and sisters, in the name of our Lord Jesus Christ, that all of you agree with one another in what you say and that there be no divisions among you, but that you be perfectly united in mind and thought," 1 Corinthians: 1:10, NIV). When we deal with animosity from race to race because of the color of our skin, it only incites more and more hatred within our country. When we as a nation can't let go of the past and live in the present by finding some kind of common ground, we are looking towards a disparaging future as a country. The American people are desensitized to America's lack of real democracy due to the overexposure of the same lies that are constantly being told by politicians just to become elected into office.

This government is not for the people; this government is only concerned with political agendas. The first step to governing should be unification.

There are so many people who have been hurt and are currently hurting to this day because of failed politicians. There are people who are literally on their deathbeds and unable to receive treatment or losing their homes and vehicles due to the lack of unification from my American government. When do we realize that all of this in some form is due to the hatred that we as Americans have towards each other? Unfortunately, this country was built on the blood and sweat from people who are viewed as threats to this country.

How do we expect to be considered a great country when, from the beginning, this land was forcefully taken by way of shedding innocent blood and society built by way of slavery?

God has not forgotten all of the damage that the powers in this country have imposed on innocent people. As I have stated, this is just the beginning of the ripple effect from all the injustices that this country has dealt to certain races of people ("For with what judgment ye judge, ye shall be judged: and with what measure ye mete, it shall be measured to you again," Matthew 7:2). This means you cannot harm people and not expect to be harmed, and you cannot enact injustice to people and then expect justice.

Sir Isaac Newton's well-known theory of gravity is that what goes up must come down. This country has to expect what it has dished out. When we think of America, we have to think of the establishment, or rather what this country was built on, which were hatred, injustice, slavery, racism, segregation, and death. This country does not have a real unifier to actually bring the American people together. It is so hard for a country that has always been separated to be unified when we have never reflected the original intent of this country.

America today is not the America it needs to be, but it takes the will of every American who has a heart of compassion to reestablish the grounds of what this country was built on because we are only as solid as our foundation when we ground ourselves in humility, reopen our hearts for compassion, wrap ourselves in love. Only then can we as a whole break the chains of hatred.

The wildfire that has spread so far throughout this country has marred what our society is supposed to look like. Why do we look at people and immediately think they are bad? ("He has made everything beautiful in its time..." Ecclesiastes 3:11). The only reason we are dealing with this invisible infirmity is because of the disobedience of mankind. When we take the blame for our own self-destruction as humans and open ourselves up for constructive criticism, we will start a new birth of a nation and be the light that we were created to be ("Ye are the light of the world. A city that is set on an hill cannot be hid. Neither do men light a candle, and put it under a bushel, but on a candlestick; and it giveth light unto all that are in the house. Let your light shine so before men, that they may see your good works, and glorify your father which is in heaven," Matthew 5:14-16).

America cannot keep perpetuating its demeaning, derogatory, vilifying, disparaging, disrespectful ways and not expect the same distraught, frenzied, hysterical, deranged America we have always been. America needs more social activists from every ethnicity who are willing to put the work in, which means there needs to be a Martin Luther King Jr. in every community in America, from whites, to blacks, to Hispanics, to Asians, and so on. We try to quote Dr. King's speeches but rarely put into action the work Dr. King put in to make the changes that we as a people are looking for because true change requires dedication, passion, and, most importantly, sacrifice.

Dr. Martin Luther King Jr. had a dream, and the reason his dream came to pass was because of the passion, dedication, and, most importantly, sacrifice he made to make his dream a reality. Even though he did not get to see his dream in the natural, he had already seen it in the spiritual because he took on the same purpose as Jesus. When he stated, "We will make it to the mountaintop", he said he might not make it there with us because his eyes have seen the glory. He knew at that point that for true change to happen, something had to be sacrificed, and he was willing, even if it had to be him.

Right to this day, his dream has been fulfilled, but it does not stop with Dr. King. We as a country have to pick up the mantle and be willing to carry it for the sake of change, for the sake of humanity, and, most of all, for the sake of love, but we cannot let the pride of life stop us from making a better life for all of our children. There is no such thing as a "white American" or "black American" or "Asian-American" or "Hispanic American" or "black folks" and "white folks" or "Asian folks" or "Hispanic folks". We are all human beings; we are all American people. This is the native Americans' home, and we are all foreigners living among them in their land. So, rather than confrontation, we all should try to live among each other in peace, without the ridicule and stereotyping of people because they are different than we are.

Diversity brings growth and evolution – is inevitable, meaning you will constantly change, whether it be good or bad. America is being challenged every day to become a better, stronger, diversified, growing nation or be the same hateful, racially motivated, stagnant country we have always been. Because when we don't stand for something, we will fall for anything, so I would rather stand for equality, justice, and righteousness than fall for bigotry, racism, and hatred. We are being tested every day due the decisions we make as individuals that can have a global impact and effect on this country.

So often, we have felt the sharp sting from the mouths of different ethnicities when they use the word "nigger" to impose control on African Americans, or the word "wetbacks" on Hispanics, as well as rednecks towards Caucasians.

Americans are attempting to diminish each other's character when we call each other these deplorable, disgraceful, reprehensible, outlandish names, which brings division amongst us as people. Americans' inclusion of its citizens is a dependency factor, meaning that the color of your skin, financial status, the way you appear, or even one's educational status are the standards or bases on which people are being judged instead of being judged on character, morality, kindness, and truthfulness. These are the things that make people good, upstanding human beings.

We are trapped as a nation because of our thought patterns. We are so trapped mentally, stuck in the same traditions as our predecessors, that we don't realize that our ancestors paved the way for us to have rights that they didn't have. They didn't give them to us by stealing, robbing, or killing. We obtain what they wanted us to have through faith, peace, and patience.

Unity is power, and division is hatred, but love is the key.

When we decide to use the tool that we have, then and only then will we unlock the door to our purpose and greatness as a country, driven by love. Then we can be an example for every nation to see. It is repugnant to think of America as the same America as it was in the 1800s or even the early 1900s because of the expansion from those times until now. This country has revolutionized so dramatically from those times to now.

It is as essential for us as a country to evolve with time as it is for us as humans to breathe.

When we stop changing, we stop breathing.

God designed us to live within Earth's ecosystems and subdue it just like he made mankind to live together in unity. God is sovereign over all, and since humanity is the similitude of a sovereign God, it is only natural for us as humans to exercise our sovereignty in the earthly realm. However, God did not create us to be supreme authorities over each other because we would be stepping into God's role, which is why Satan was cast down. There is only one Supreme Being over everything and everybody. God is seen more through his creation in love and unity because us together as one shows the adversary how big our God is and the magnitude of authority He has.

If we would use Jesus Christ as the model and the standard for this country, this country would be the America it should be instead of the America that it is imposing hatred, racism, violence, anger, division, and death on its citizens, which only exacerbates the ongoing problems that the American people are dealing with.

We have been wired since birth to establish segregation in many things.

We only deal with people who look like us or live in the same areas. It is totally inexplicable how the constitution is only enforced according to one's ethnicity or color when the constitution is supposed to be for every American, which tells me that since the constitution was written up by a certain group or ethnicity, certain ethnicities feel as though it only applies to them and view every other ethnicity as inferior, so America has always endorsed this divisiveness from the beginning.

I encourage the American people to become better.

This nation has not inadvertently disregarded the civil rights of its citizens; everything that has been done has all been very intentional, as well as strategically planned. America has been torn and divided, which only perpetuates adversity and calamity. Moreover, America as a whole is diminishing throughout its inner cities because of the violence that comes from division, such as gang affiliation and fully stratified social groups and neighborhoods. We are being brainwashed every day by local politicians, judges, as well as police officers. Justice is now rarely given but rather bought. The corruption and division that this country has condoned for so many years can be seen through the day-to-day lives of its citizens, some more clearly than others. The national anthem is about freedom while the nation in question routinely and systematically oppresses certain citizens ("In righteousness shalt thou be established; thou shall be far from oppression; for thou shalt not fear: and from terror; for it shall not come near thee," Isaiah 54:14). We are all victims of the war that we are fighting within ourselves, the war between love and hatred, which manifests outwardly by how we treat each other.

When I treat you badly as a person, call you out of your name, and spew hate towards a race or individual, it only speaks to the insecurities that I have towards myself as a person and member of a race.

When you truly love yourself inside and out, it will be displayed outwardly in how you treat people! People are holding on to tradition, which makes them hateful and bitter towards others because that's all they know to do and how they have been raised ("But he answered and said unto them, Why do ye also transgress the commandment of God for your tradition?" Matthew 15:3). We have to rebuild the foundation of America by turning down racism and hatred in favor of the love of Jesus Christ ("Consequently, you are no longer strangers and foreigners, but fellow citizens with the God's people and also members of his household, built on the foundation of the apostles and prophets, with Christ Jesus himself as the chief cornerstone; In him the whole building is joined together and rises to become a holy temple in the Lord: And in him you too are being built together to become a dwelling in which God lives by his Spirit," Ephesians 2:19-22).

When we replace the hatred that has hardened the heart of mankind with the love that we were created from and walk in the humility of grace, we will expose the vulnerabilities of the adversary. When his tactics are revealed, it prepares us better to be able to deal with him, and one of the tactics he's always used has been division. We have become more cognizant of the missteps of this great country and the residue of its evil-doing. The other tactic that he has manipulated humanity with is hatred. By these two means of persuasion, he has brought on so much chaos, hurt, and death. He has torn apart so many families, so many friendships, and held so many people hostage mentally. By these means of coercion, we have been forced into life-styles that are completely different than what was originally intended for humanity. America has been shamed because of our lack of unification, as well as lack of love for mankind, but America, through perseverance and determination to be better people as well as better Americans, can overcome any adversity that will keep us from becoming better human beings. If we do, we will become the great Americans that we have sworn to become ("For as he thinketh in his heart, so is he..." Proverbs 23:7).

Americans are not always made to understand our own inclinations and proclivities, and the reason for those inclinations and proclivities, so we don't find value in questioning why different people have the tendency or urge to act a certain way, like when black people naturally run from police officers. Black people so often die over the smallest encounters with police officers. Equivocation about the division and racism in this country that have been disguised or camouflaged to the point that we would rather it not be discussed is harmful. We have been propelled into another direction to become a better nation. There is so much animosity coming from all the ethnicities living amongst each other within this country.

We are being distracted, diverted, and deflected from the truth.

There is so much anguish, agony, sorrow, and grief among the American people due to the tragedies, calamities, and catastrophes that different families have endured from violent and hateful people, which only stems from racism and some diabolical form of hatred.

The only panacea for America's dysfunctional society is love ("Though I speak with the tongues of men and of angels, and have not charity, I am become as sounding brass, or a tinkling cymbal. And though I have the gift of prophecy, and understand all mysteries, and all knowledge; and though I have all faith, so that I could remove mountains, and have not charity, I am nothing. And though I bestow all my goods to feed the poor, and though I give my body to be burned, and have not charity, it profiteth me nothing. Charity suffereth long, and is kind;

Charity envieth not; charity vaunteth not itself, is not puffed up, Doth not behave itself unseemly, seeketh not her own, is not easily provoked, thinketh no evil; Rejoiceth not in iniquity, but rejoiceth in the truth: Beareth all things, believeth all things, hopeth all things, endureth all things," 1 Corinthians 13:1-7).

Miracles happen when we begin to love one another the way God loves us as individual prized possessions instead of racially motivated hateful divided groups and learn to seek the will of the Creator. The preposterous, absurd, analytical tactics that this government uses to brainwash American citizens and keep us divided are to keep the poor poorer and the rich richer. No one at the top really cares about the homeless people of this country because the homeless don't possess the same attributes as the people who are at the top. It doesn't matter to them that they don't have food because if that was so, then there would be a government-funded homeless shelter and food bank in every state in the United States, and there would be some type of policy put together from the lawmakers on Capitol Hill for healthcare for the homeless because they are still a part of this country as well.

However, they would rather those people die off so Americans tax dollars can go towards looking into the corruption of these dirty, so-called businessmen and politicians who are still allowed to hold their positions, even though by legal and federal law some should be in jail, and this is just some of the reason why we are living in a separated nation, which is grounded in hatred and racism. The contempt that this country has for some of its citizens because of the color of our skin or our ancestral background or ethnicity is very degrading as human beings ("What causes fights and quarrels among you? Don't they come from your desires that battle within you? You covet but you cannot get what you want, so you quarrel and fight. You do not have because you do not ask God. When you ask, you do not receive, because you ask with wrong motives, that you may spend what you get on your pleasures," James 4:1-3, NIV).

When we as a people line our lives up with the truth, which is the word of God, then we will start to positively impact the lives of the people that surround us, the people that we love.

The constant preparations that we must make as Americans to grow, as well as to train up the next generation to break the cycle of bigotry, racism, and hatred, must be orchestrated constantly to dampen the reoccurrence of such deplorable, reprehensible, disgraceful character traits that so many of us possess. We have been immersed so deeply within the confinements of our own races that we fail to see the damage that we cause to different races in our society. It is my prayer that the adversity that we as Americans go through to live amongst each other from a diversified aspect is to become more and more revolutionized.

As we evolve, the dissolution of racism in this country should be forever concluded. When we learn to assimilate different cultures and ethnicities, we will stabilize the fundamental core of humanity. The dissimulation of fundamentalism from different religious perspectives should not take place because what makes me different from you also makes me respect you as an individual. No one should be killed for their beliefs because one day we will all be judged by the One who created us all ("Brothers and sisters, do not slander one another. Anyone who speaks against a brother or sister or judges them speaks against the law and judges it. When you judge the law, you are not keeping it, but sitting in judgment on it. There is only one Lawgiver and Judge, the one who is able to save and destroy. But you – who are you to judge your neighbor?" James 4:11-12, NIV).

The presumptuous behavior that solidifies discrimination in the U.S. is rooted in the vagueness or uncertainty of the moral standard for how to treat all people instead of certain people. This country has polarized its citizens by race or ethnicity for years. We have tried segregation, and we've seen how that only diminishes society. Predominantly, America is supposed to be the standard for what other nations are striving to become, but it seems that this nation has missed the mark for the standard for morality and human decency.

I do not vilify this great country, but I do vilify the terms and conditions that this country was built upon and grounded in.

The defiance and disallowance from the conditions that certain people have been bound and held in have been physically and mentally catastrophic, which have set the pattern of "hate wave" throughout American society. The imperfections that we have as a nation should be realigned and recalibrated so we can come together as one, which would require nonpartisan impartiality.

The indifference we show for human life in this country is proof that that we bestow less value on human life than that of an animal.

We have no value because we've never felt valued.

Until we realize our worth as humans to the One who created us and went to the cross for us to be redeemed after the price of sin was paid by his blood at Calvary, we will never really understand our value ("Are not two sparrows sold for a farthing? and one of them shall not fall on the ground without your Father. But the very hairs of your head are all numbered. Fear ye not therefore, ye are of more value than many sparrows," Matthew 10:29-31).

The complacency that different races adopt in this country is abhorrent, horrifying, and despicable within the realm of humanity.

I am pontificating about egregious acts that Americans witness and the natural disparity between the experiences of different racial groups from the time of slavery until today's era. Life as an American is great, despite of some of the adversities that we have had to overcome. No matter how we look at it, we have come a great way from where we were, but we still have a way to go to grow and become a great, unified nation. I pray that the next generation of Americans can become more understanding and sensitive to each other and never forget what the people before them had to go through just for being who they were.

I declare that America will become a better nation and be unified with one faith, one baptism, one son, one spirit, and one God ("The Lord is my shepherd; I shall not want. He maketh me to lie down in green pastures: he leadeth me beside the still waters. He restoreth my soul: he leadeth me in the paths of righteousness for his name's sake. Yea, though I walk through the valley of the shadow of death, I will fear no evil: for thou art with me; thy rod and thy staff they comfort me. Thou preparest a table before me in the presence of mine enemies: thou anointest my head with oil; my cup runneth over. Surely goodness and mercy shall follow me all the days of my life: and I will dwell in the house of the Lord forever..." Psalm 23-24).

We as children of God can live together and love each other from pure hearts.

That will make the world great again.

Final Thoughts

...

I pray to the God of all creation that my personal experiences and my life's testimonies inspire and change the thought patterns of anyone who reads my book. I personally thank God for every experience that I've had because they all have helped transform me into a better person. Through experience, things that I didn't previously understand are much more understandable to me.

I've learned that prayer is a very powerful tool, one that God has given humanity through the bloodshed of His son, our Lord and savior Jesus Christ, that we may come boldly to the throne of grace and petition to God our cares and wants.

Through faith, if we believe, it shall be done.

ABOUT THE AUTHOR

PATRICK BAKER is a graduate of Foreman High School and was raised in Foreman, Arkansas. He loves to give back to his community through serving food and donating clothes and shoes at homeless shelters. He is very family oriented and hard working. Patrick is excited about this journey as a new author!

J. Kenkade
PUBLISHING®

Our Motto
"Transforming Life Stories"

Also Available from
J. Kenkade Publishing

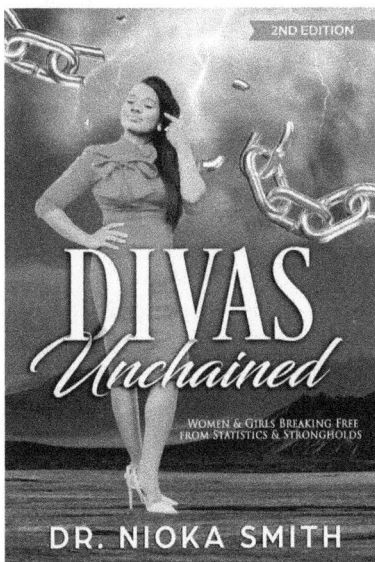

ISBN: 978-1-944486-25-9
Visit www.drniokasmith.com
Author: Dr. Nioka Smith

Sexually abused by her father at the age of 14, pregnant at the age of 17, and a nervous breakdown at the age of 28, Dr. Nioka Smith's painful past almost killed her, until the voice of the Lord guided her into destroying strongholds and reversing Satan's plan for her life. DIVAS Unchained is the powerful chain-breaking reality of the many unfortunate strongholds our women and girls face. Dr. Nioka uses her divine gift to help women and girls break free from destructive life cycles and prosper in all areas of life. Satan has lied to you. It's time to expose his lies. It's time to break free!

Also Available from
J. Kenkade Publishing

J. KENKADE PUBLISHING PRESENTS

THE *Face* OF
THE *New*
ENGINEER

Dr. Lashun K. Massey

ISBN: 978-1-944486-53-2
Visit www.jkenkadepublishing.com
Author: Dr. Lashun K. Massey

This autobiography provides an account of the life of Dr. Lashun King Massey, P.E. It outlines the challenges that she faced growing up as a child in rural Arkansas. Although Dr. Massey was born in a socioeconomically depressed area in Arkansas, she managed to defy the odds and pursue a career in engineering. This book helps shed on light Dr. Massey's childhood and uncover the challenges that she faced in pursuing a career in engineering.

Also Available from
J. Kenkade Publishing

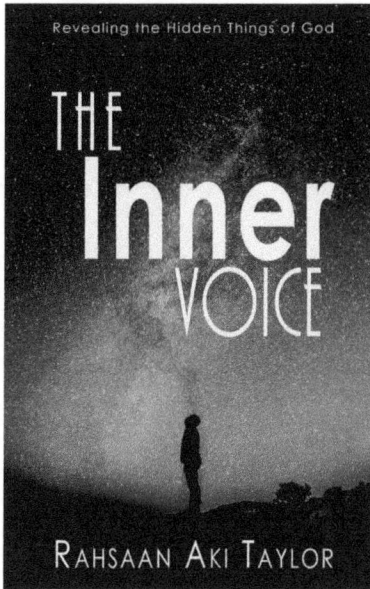

ISBN: 978-1-944486-12-9
Visit www.jkenkadepublishing.com
Author: Rahsaan Aki Taylor

We all have wondered why bad things happen to us or someone we love. Often times, we never receive the answer to the questions that are asked. Therefore, the content of this book enlightens you on many topics and situations. It will expose the unknown. Once you begin to read this book of knowledge you will not be able to put it down. It is guaranteed to have you on the edge of your seat. It teaches how to prevent failures and mishaps. It will have you alert at all times and will reveal some of the hidden things of God.

Also Available from
J. Kenkade Publishing

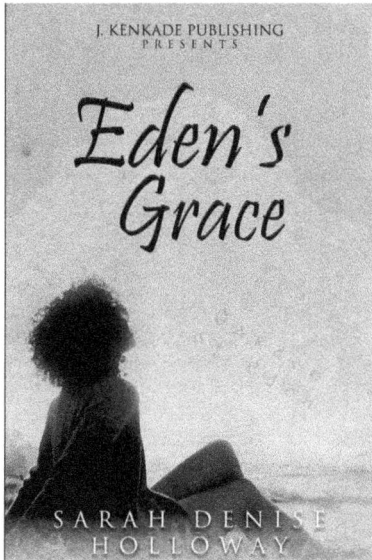

ISBN: 978-1-944486-29-7
Visit www.jkenkadepublishing.com
Author: Sarah Denise Holloway

Eden isn't a complicated girl, but she's been hurt by people that should have been more apt to protect her. She's struggling with who she is what her purpose is, but who isn't? Eden's life is suddenly turned upside down when her Aunt Liza, the staple matriarch keeping the family together is dying and Eden has no idea how to come to grips with the past that threatens her future. Will Eden understand her purpose before her aunts passing, or will time run out for the both of them? Laugh, cry, and fight alongside Eden in this touching and riveting story of pain, loss, and love and learn to find God's grace in the midst of it all.

This page intentionally left blank.

J. Kenkade Publishing